So
Vegetables

Written by Jill Mitchell
Illustrated by Andrea Jaretzki

A carrot.

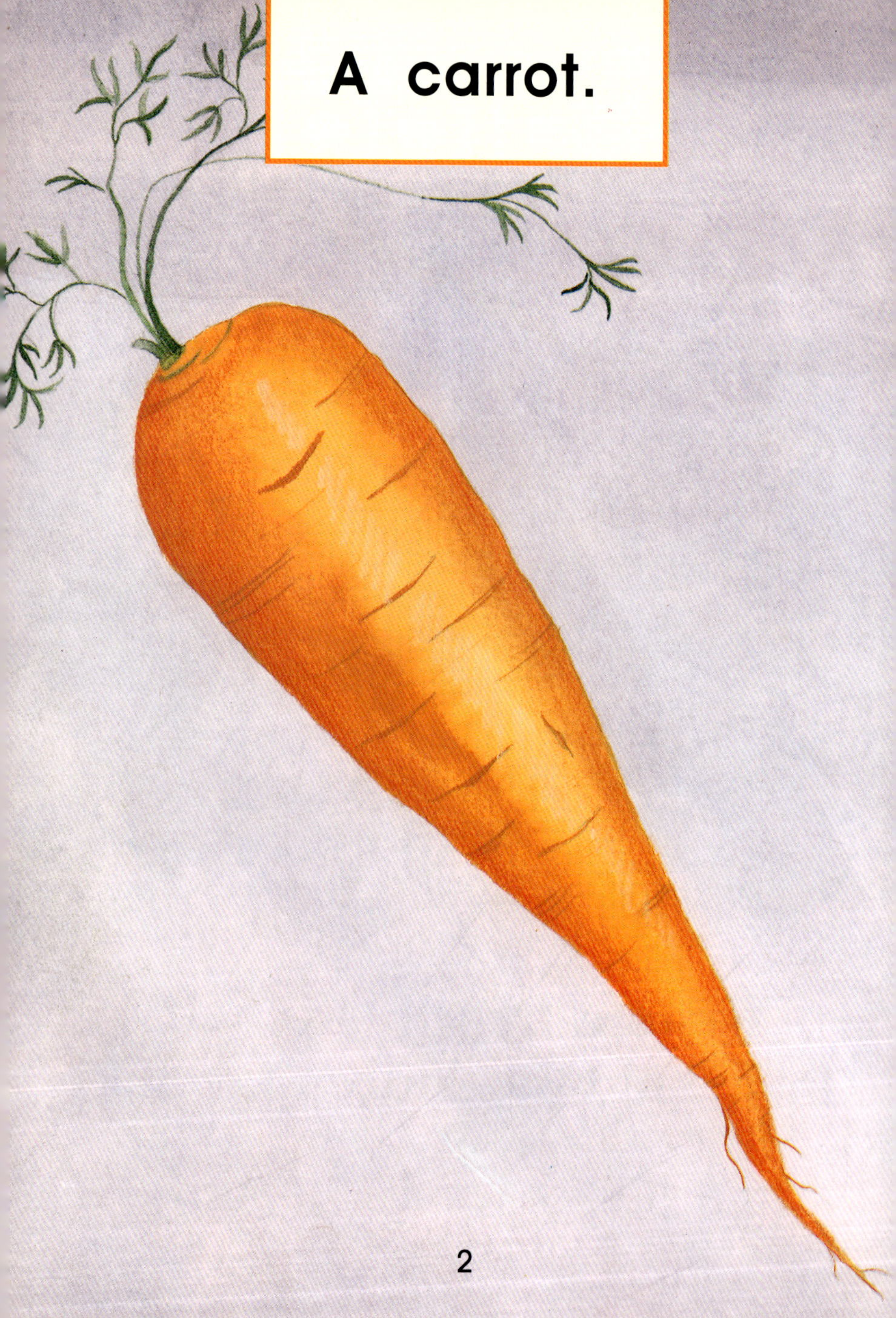

A lettuce.

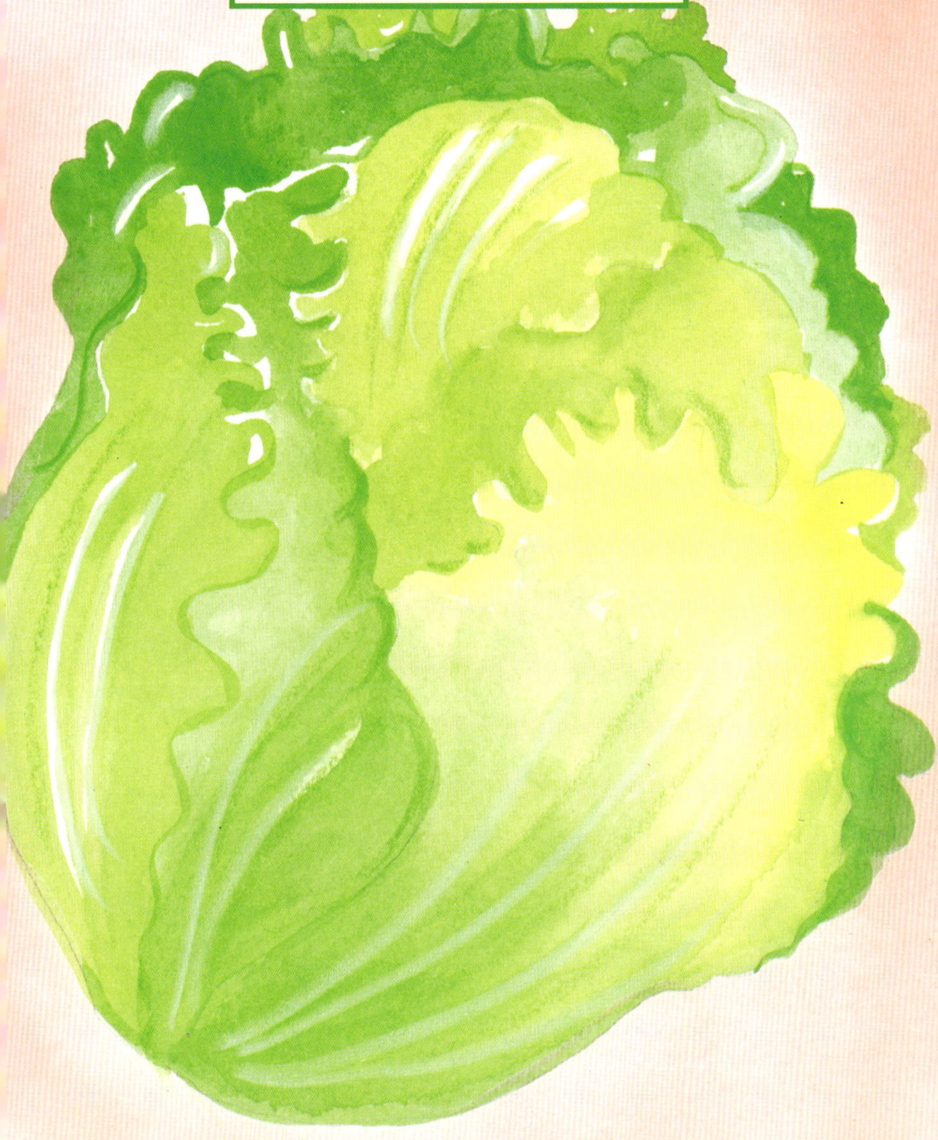

A tomato.

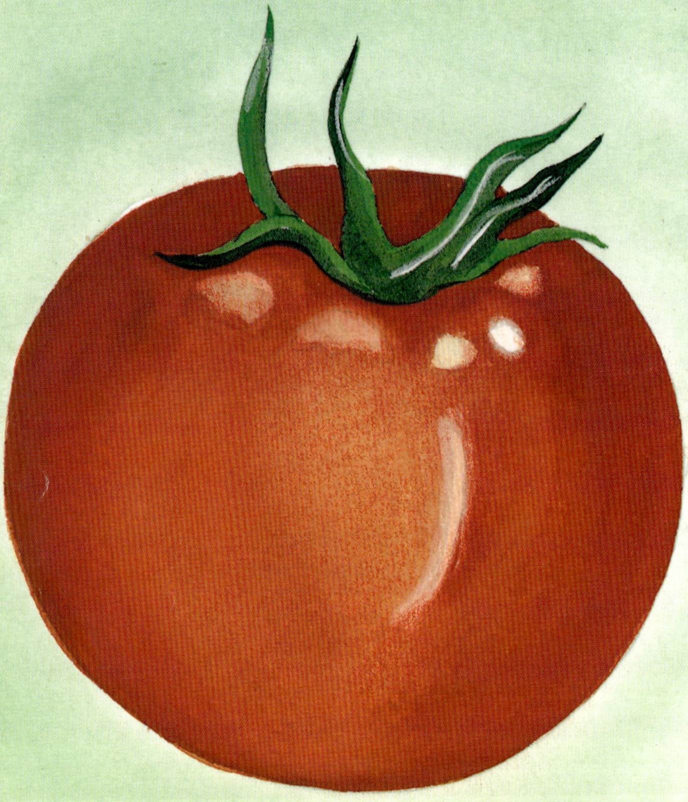

A cucumber.

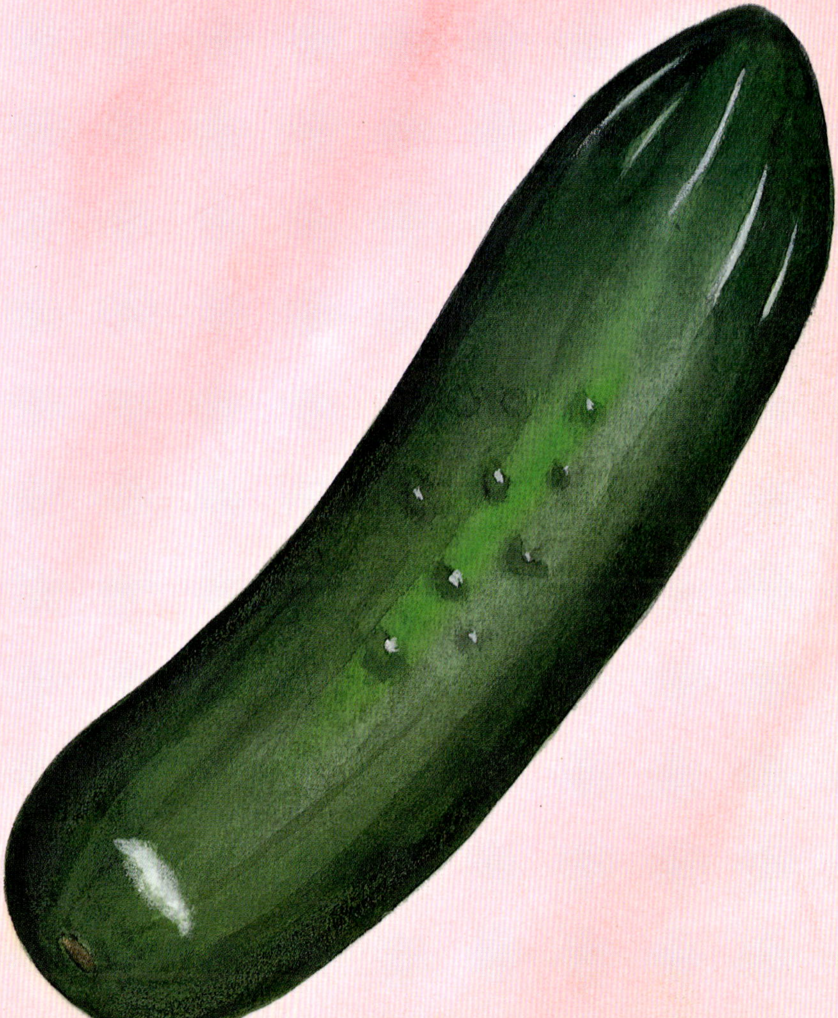

A radish.

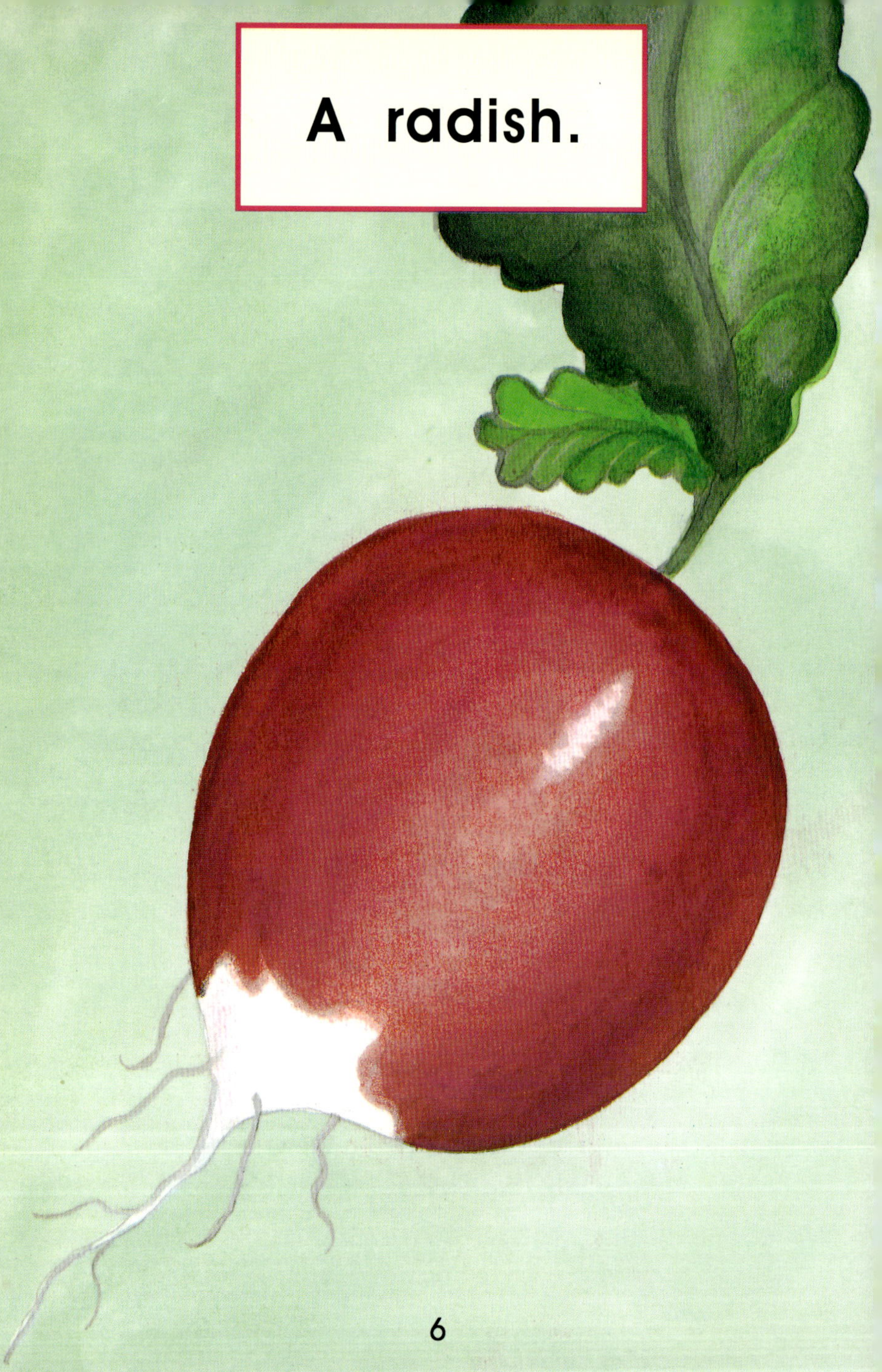

A green onion.

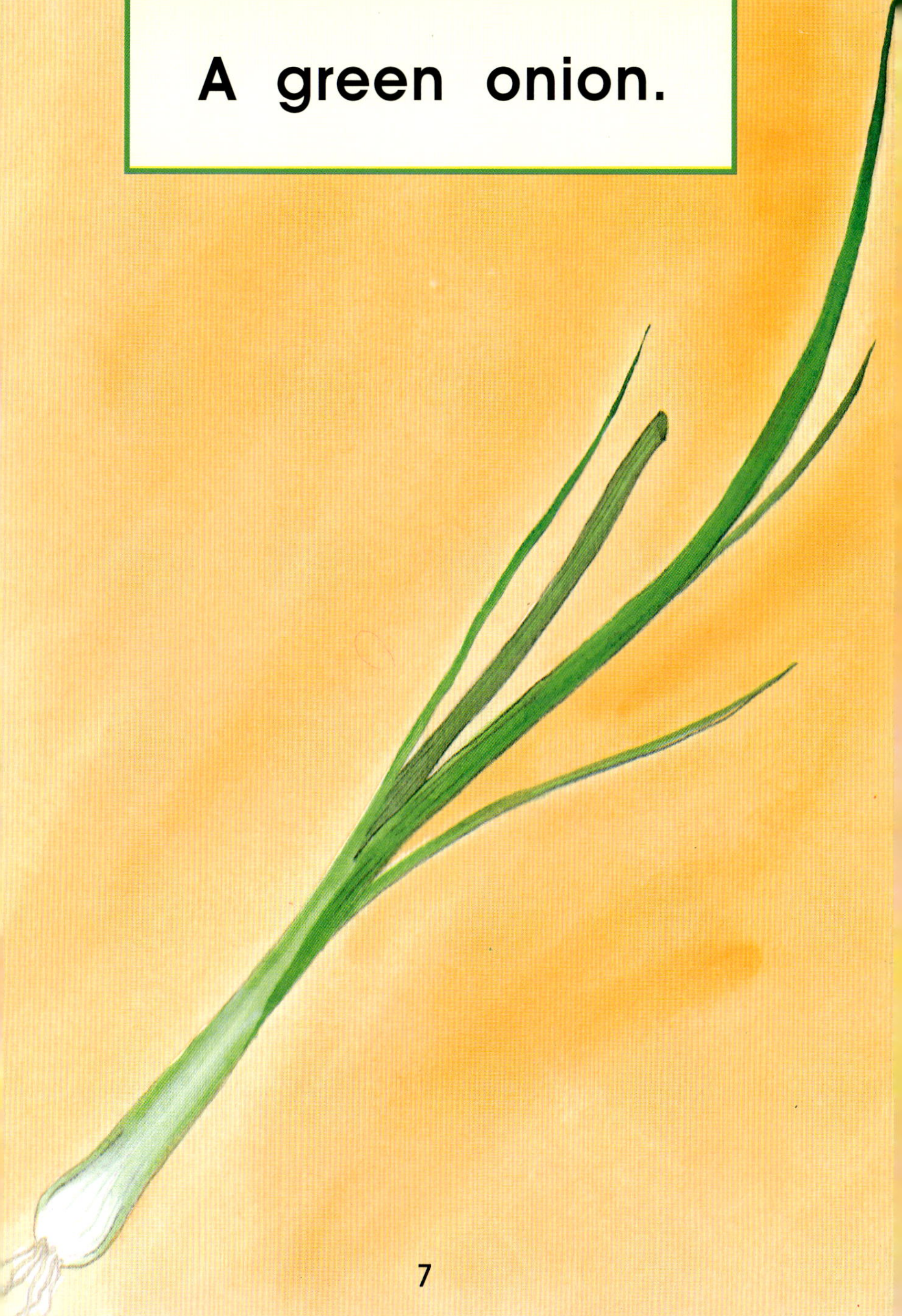

A salad!

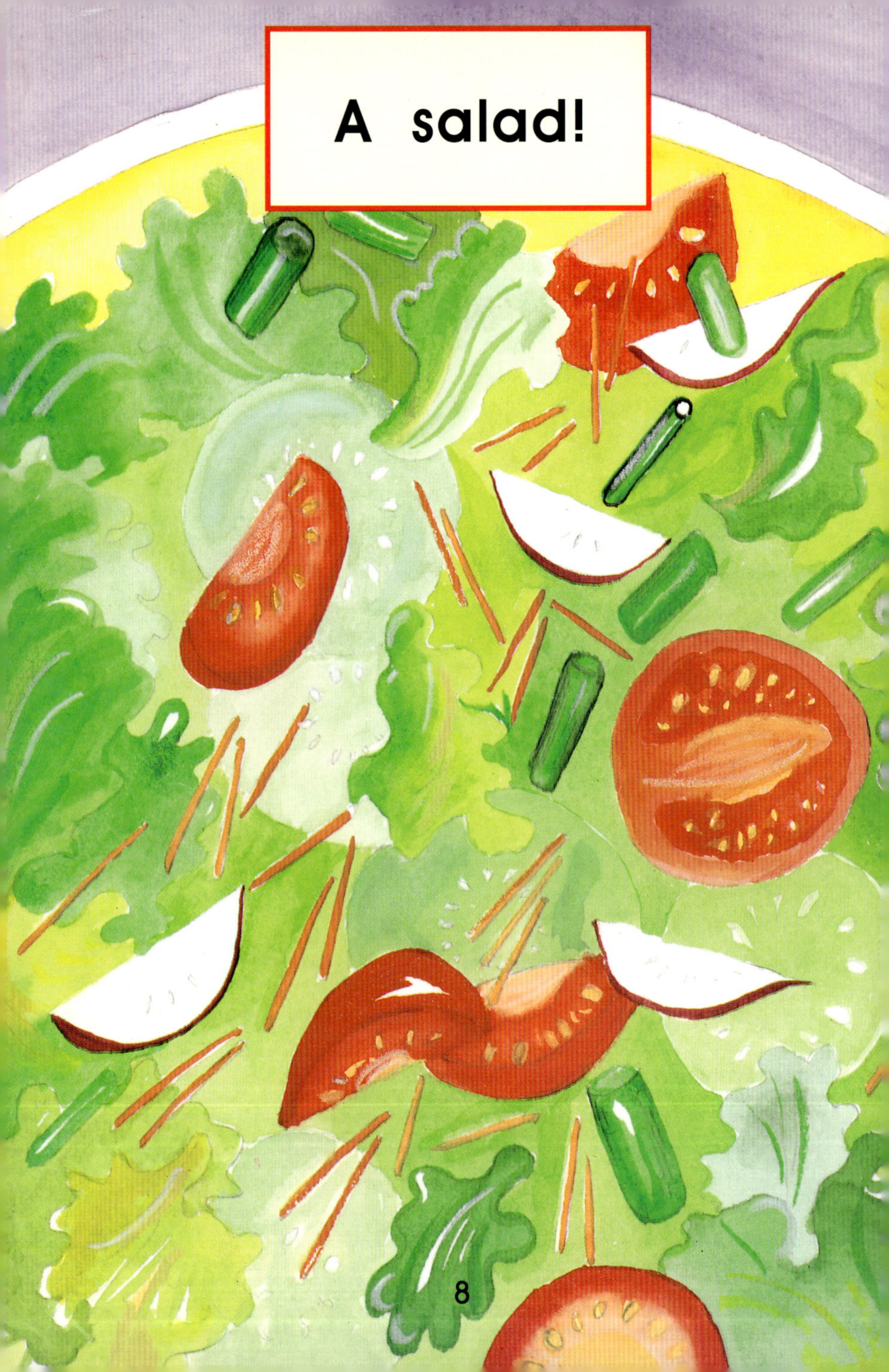